Let's hold on to the
confession of our hope
without wavering, because
the one who made the
promises is reliable.

Hebrews 10:23

The

of Christmas

A Daily Devotional for Advent

Rachel Gilmore
&
Kay Kotan

Market
Square
BOOKS

The

Voices

of Christmas

A Daily Devotional for Advent

©2021 Market Square Publishing, LLC

books@marketsquarebooks.com
P.O. Box 23664 Knoxville, Tennessee 37933
ISBN: 978-1-950899-36-4

Printed and Bound in the United States of America
Cover Illustration & Book Design ©2021 Market Square Publishing, LLC

Editor: Kristin Lighter • Post-Process Editor: Ken Rochelle

Scripture quotations taken from the
following versions of the Bible:

CEB
Scripture quotations from the COMMON ENGLISH BIBLE.
© Copyright 2011 COMMON ENGLISH BIBLE. All rights reserved.
Used by permission. (www.CommonEnglishBible.com).

CEV
Scripture quotations from the Contemporary English Version®
Copyright © 1995 American Bible Society. All rights reserved.

ESV
Scriptures marked ESV are taken from the THE HOLY BIBLE, ENGLISH STANDARD
VERSION (ESV): Scriptures taken from THE HOLY BIBLE, ENGLISH STANDARD
VERSION ® Copyright© 2001 by Crossway, a publishing ministry of Good News Publishers.
Used by permission.

NIV
Scriptures marked NIV are taken from the NEW INTERNATIONAL VERSION (NIV):
Scripture taken from THE HOLY BIBLE, NEW INTERNATIONAL VERSION ®.
Copyright ©1973, 1978, 1984, 2011 by Biblica, Inc.™. Used by permission of Zondervan.

NRSV
New Revised Standard Version Bible, copyright © 1989
National Council of the Churches of Christ in the United States of America.
Used by permission. All rights reserved worldwide.

TLB
Scriptures marked TLB are taken from the THE LIVING BIBLE (TLB): Scripture
taken from THE LIVING BIBLE copyright© 1971. Used by permission of Tyndale
House Publishers, Inc., Carol Stream, Illinois 60188. All rights reserved.

TM
Scriptures marked TM are taken from the The Message: THE BIBLE IN CONTEM-
PORARY ENGLISH, copyright©1993, 1994, 1995, 1996, 2000, 2001, 2002.
Used by permission of NavPress Publishing Group

Table of Contents

Week Four – Experience and Joy 75

Sunday • Fourth Sunday of Advent
Monday • Elizabeth
Tuesday • Mary
Wednesday • Joseph
Thursday • Shepherds
Friday • Wise men
Saturday • Reflection

Postscript. 99

A Plan of HOPE

    Healing
    Opportunity
    Peace
    Experience

Introduction

Are you ready yet? Advent is a time to get ready to celebrate the birth of Christ. While many of us look forward to the activities of Christmas – from caroling to decorating Christmas trees and finding the perfect gift for someone special – the best gift we can give to God and ourselves is to take time each day to focus on what this season is all about.

Christ's birth was so important and transformational because when God came to earth as a baby, hope was born anew in all of us. Because of Jesus' birth, life, death and resurrection, we have hope that when we face stressful, anxious, or painful times, that healing, love, peace and joy will find us again. Because of hope, we know that light and life and love will have the final word.

Our gift to you this Advent season is a daily devotional to help you explore the theme of hope more deeply. We are inviting you to join us on this journey of HOPE towards Christmas. Each week you will be offered a deeper insight into one of the four elements of HOPE:

- During the first week, we will focus on **H**ealing.
- During week two, we will look at **O**pportunities, especially opportunities to give and receive love.
- During week three, we will learn more about **P**eace.
- In the final week, we will explore **E**xperiences of joy.

We will look at these themes through the unique journey of six prominent characters– or a group of characters' voices – in the Christmas story. On the first day of each week you will be introduced to the theme and scripture of the week. On days two through six, we will look at the theme through the lenses of the characters and their voices, then offering reflective questions. On the seventh day of each week, you will find a summary of the week, as well as additional questions for your personal reflection or processing in your small group.

Advent can be a busy season for so many of us, with parties to attend, presents to buy and meals to prepare. Our prayer for you is that you see this Advent season as a unique journey. Take time each day to slow down and explore these elements of HOPE, and by doing so, find hope born anew in you this year!

With love for you on this journey,

Kay and Rachel

WEEK ONE

Healing and Hope

11-27

First Sunday of Advent

"... in his name, the nations will put their hope."
Matthew 12:21 (NIV)

The Greek word for hope is ἐλπίς which means
to anticipate or expect something that you are
sure will happen. We often have anticipations and
expectations when we are planning for a journey or
are on a journey. The journey towards Christmas is
no exception. Sometimes we bring "baggage" with
us on a journey filled with items we believe we will
need along the way.   On life's journey, we often carry
damaged "baggage" that we hope will be healed. It
might be pain, struggle, doubt, or grief.

When it comes to healing, how can we have hope
that it will really happen, how can we be certain? We
serve a God who created the world and humanity to
not face illness, brokenness or death. With the fall
of Adam and Eve, the need for healing was born and
Jesus came to ensure that we will all experience
complete healing, in this life or in the life to come.

There is a lot of uncertainty in the world and it can be hard to hope in many things, but when it comes to our hope in God, we can be certain that we serve a good God who wants us to experience healing and wholeness in this lifetime or the one to come. This week we will look at how we can experience healing and hope as we examine the lives of John the Baptist, Mary, Joseph, the shepherds and the Magi.

Reflections from Day One

1. What "baggage" (i.e., grief, hurt, pain, struggle, doubt) do you have that needs to be healed?

2. Is there any baggage that you give to God but continuously take back? What is it, and why do you believe you might not trust God to carry your baggage for you?

3. What are you hoping for in this Advent season?

Monday

John the Baptist

> *"I'm baptizing you here in the river, turning your old life in for a kingdom life. The real action comes next: The main character in this drama – compared to him I'm a mere stagehand – will ignite the kingdom life within you, a fire within you, the Holy Spirit within you, changing you from the inside out. He's going to clean house – make a clean sweep of your lives. He'll place everything true in its proper place before God; everything false he'll put out with the trash to be burned."*
>
> **Matthew 3:11-2 (TM)**

I can only imagine the strange looks that John the Baptist would receive when people showed up to see this fiery preacher in the wilderness wearing camel hair and eating locusts and honey. But his message of preparing for God's arrival by repenting and receiving the gift of baptism is a powerful one. As a pastor, I always thought that Advent was a great season to be baptized because it reminds us that we are all broken and in need of God's abundant grace. It's a reminder that, in baptism, our souls are cleansed and prepared for the gift of the Holy Spirit to come and dwell in us. But it can be scary to give God complete control of your life and have access to all of you.

So many of us have been hurt, and our need for healing runs deep. When I read the story of John the Baptist, I'm reminded that sometimes the first step is admitting that I need help and that I can't fix myself. The next step is to rely on God's plan for my healing instead of controlling the process myself.

Advent is a great time to reflect on the areas where we need God's help and to remind ourselves to let God have full access to our hearts and lives for true healing to occur. It's also a time to celebrate that John the Baptist was just preparing the way for the coming of Christ, who will give us the passion we need to live the lives we are called to live. Is God calling you to be a "John the Baptist" to someone in your life? Is God trying to use you to help other people know Jesus?

Reflections from Day Two

1. Where might you need help from God in healing that only God can provide?

2. Where might you be holding back your whole heart from God, and why?

3. Is God calling you to be a "John the Baptist" for someone in this season? If so, who and what is the next step?

Tuesday

Mary

Good morning!
You're beautiful with God's beauty,
Beautiful inside and out!
God be with you.

She was thoroughly shaken, wondering what was behind a greeting like that. But the angel assured her, "Mary, you have nothing to fear. God has a surprise for you: You will become pregnant and give birth to a son and call his name Jesus.

Luke 1:28-29 (TM)

Can you imagine this scene? Can you imagine standing in the shoes of Mary at this moment? An Angel, Gabriel, appears to Mary. He calls out her inner and outer beauty. Just an Angel appearing is one thing, but imagine this type of greeting. Even before Gabriele shared the "surprise," Mary was already shaken. Then Gabriel springs the big news, the "surprise," on her. In addition to wondering how

13

this could happen, she must have been wondering, "Why me?" And, I can't help but think she was also wondering how she was going to tell her fiance, Joseph, about this "surprise."

Furthermore, Mary had to be wondering if Joseph would bolt out of their relationship because of this "surprise." There is a whole lot to fear: the appearance of an Angel, the greeting, the news of the "surprise," how the surprise had come about, how to tell Joseph, and how all of this would affect her upcoming nuptials with Joseph. All of this, not to mention how she would tell her parents.

Mary is so faithful and poised, especially when you consider that her estimated age when she conceived was between 12 and 16. While her initial response was fear, she quickly moved to praise. In Luke 1:38(CEB), Mary leans into her faith and says, "Let it be with me just as you have said."

She trusted in the Lord. When she shared the news with Elizabeth, she explained that the Lord had looked upon her with high favor because the Lord had done such great things for her. Mary turned a circumstance that would paralyze some into an opportunity to praise and glorify God. This is remarkable considering how self-centered teenagers can sometimes be.

As we enter this holy time of Advent focusing on hope, what are you carrying that needs healing? What fears from your life's journey are keeping you from living a life of hope and joy? How can you lean into your faith a little more and release your fears, anxieties, worries, and hurts into the hope of Jesus Christ? What will you turn over to Christ to promote your healing leading to the hope of this Advent season and the new year that is approaching?

Reflections from Day Three

1. Have you ever experienced a time when you wondered, "Why me?" What words come to mind when you reflect on that experience?

2. How did you come to reconcile and recognize yourself as the chosen one?

3. What did you learn about yourself in this experience that you continue to carry?

Wednesday

Joseph

> *While he was trying to figure a way out, he had a*
> *dream. God's angel spoke in the dream: "Joseph,*
> *son of David, don't hesitate to get married. Mary's*
> *pregnancy is Spirit-conceived. God's Holy Spirit*
> *has made her pregnant. She will bring a son to*
> *birth, and when she does, you, Joseph, will name*
> *him Jesus – 'God saves' – because he will save*
> *his people from their sins." This would bring the*
> *prophet's embryonic revelation to full term: Watch*
> *for this – a virgin will get pregnant and bear a son;*
> *They will name him Immanuel (Hebrew for "God*
> *is with us").*
>
> **Matthew 1:20-23 (TM)**

In the scripture above, Mary has shared the
"surprise" (her pregnancy) with Joseph. Can you
imagine what kind of "story" it sounded like when
Mary told Joseph? I can only imagine that when
Joseph was trying to process all of this, he thought
something like this:

So let me get this right. Mary tells me she is going
to have a baby. Now, I know we haven't been

intimate. And she tells me she had not been with another man. Then, she wants me to believe that the "spirit" made her pregnant. Are you kidding me? How crazy of a story is that? Does she think I am going to believe that tall tale? I have got to find a way out of this.

But God steps in and handles it, like always. God's angel spoke to Joseph in his dream. He confirmed everything Mary had told him, including the huge role this miracle baby would have in the world. When Joseph woke from the dream, he did as the Angel commanded and took Mary as his wife.

We have no way of knowing the time lapse between when Mary told Joseph the news and when God's angel spoke to Joseph in his dream. Whether it was hours or days, that time had to be incredibly difficult. Can't you just imagine him pacing back and forth in his room trying to figure out what to do? Surely, he wondered how he could get out of that relationship but not humiliate her in the process. But it all turned on a dime in a dream.

Rather than trying to get out of the relationship, he began to understand (as much as he could at the time) the roles that he and Mary would play in this life-changing event. He leaned into his faith, turning from one of the most anxious times in his life into a time of hope.

Think of a time in your life's journey when your initial conclusions about a situation took you to a dark, anxious, or fearful place. Our imaginations and assumptions are often far worse than reality. How will you lean further on hope and less on fear during this Christmas season?

Reflections from Day Four

1. When have you been surprised at how God has shown up in unbelievable ways?

2. How were you convinced they were of God?

3. We often refer to the birth of Jesus as the Miracle of Christmas or sometimes the Magic of Christmas. How will you lean more into hope – and less into fear – in this Advent season?

Thursday

Shepherds

There were shepherds camping in the neighborhood.

They had set night watches over their sheep.

Suddenly, God's angel stood among them and God's glory blazed around them.

They were terrified. The angel said, "Don't be afraid."

Luke 2:8-9 (TM)

Once again, fear is mentioned as part of the shepherd's opening scene in this story. It was not only fear, but the above scripture translation refers to the shepherds as being terrified. Here they were, in the fields guarding their sheep in the night. It was just a typical night after a normal workday. Then suddenly, their whole world changed when God's angel appeared sharing that their Savior had been born. The baby could be found wrapped in rags in a manger.

What? The Savior - swaddled in rags - lying in a

livestock feeder? I can imagine one shepherd rolling over and asking his shepherd friend if he saw and heard that, too. What did we eat for dinner tonight that would give us those crazy illusions? When they looked at one another and agreed they all heard the same thing, they just had to check to see if they were dreaming. They all decided they had to see this with their own eyes.

When they found Mary, Joseph, and baby Jesus, the shepherds shared what the angel had said. Mary listened carefully as yet again the divine plan was confirmed. The shepherds praised God and repeated the story to the amazement of others.

We have all heard that if it is too good to be true, it probably is. I am sure the shepherds had heard the same thing. We are often so ready to dismiss or minimize the goodness in our lives and others. If something good does occur, we are anticipating when the "other shoe will drop." Do you live a life expecting goodness or one that leans more towards skepticism? Do we see potential and possibility, or do we see danger and disappointment?

In this Christmas season and looking towards the new year, how will you lean on the abundant, fearless life that God has in store for all of us? How will you strive for a hope-filled rather than a hope-less outlook in this season?

Reflections from Day Five

1. "Fear not" is mentioned in the Bible approximately 366 times. That's enough to fill a calendar year. What fears would you like to lay aside in this Advent season?

2. How would this Advent season be more joyful if you were truly able to lay aside this fear?

3. How would your life change if you were able to hand over that fear to Jesus completely?

Friday

Wise Men

Then they opened their luggage and presented gifts: gold, frankincense, myrrh.

Matthew 2:11b (NIV)

We have a tradition in my family. Every year my husband and I buy the kids three gifts to open on Christmas morning. That's right, only three. Why? Because Christmas is about celebrating Jesus' birthday, and if the wise men only brought three gifts for the Christ child, then that should probably be enough gifts for our kids, too. And the gifts of gold, frankincense and myrrh are a model for the kinds of gifts we buy to open on Christmas morning.

Gold was expensive and valuable, so our kids ask for one gift that might cost a little more or be the one thing they really want for Christmas. Frankincense was burned in the temple as a sacred incense, so for the "frankincense" gift, we buy our children something that brings a spiritual fragrance to their life. It might be a candle or a devotional or prayer beads or a meditation jar, but the gift is meant to emphasize the importance of faith. Myrrh was tree sap used to make an oil that Moses used to anoint the tabernacle, and it was later used to anoint the bodies of those who had died. So the myrrh gift for our children is something that cares for their bodies, which are a living sanctuary for God (1 Corinthians 6:19). We might buy them a new pair of shoes or get them sports equipment or a spa kit, anything to remind them to take care of their bodies.

During this season of Advent, think about the gifts that could bring you hope or healing this year. Are you caring for your body, heart, and soul? What would your gold, frankincense and myrrh gifts be? Sometimes we get caught up in the commercialization of Christmas instead of being intentional about what matters most. Spend some time looking over your Christmas shopping list and select gifts that bring others closer to Christ this year.

Reflections from Day Six

1. What personal gift of healing or gift for your body might you consider giving yourself this Advent season?

2. What personal gift of hope or gift for your soul might you consider giving yourself this Advent season?

3. What personal gift to care for your spirit or your heart might you consider giving yourself this Advent season?

Saturday

Healing & Hope

Week One Summary, Reflection, & Questions

This week has been a journey of healing through the eyes of hope. Each of the key people in the story of Jesus' birth had unique journeys. Each had some sort of doubt, fear, hurt, or disappointment in need of healing. In the end, that healing was found in the hope of Jesus Christ, sent by God in human form to teach, lead, and pay the ultimate price for our sins.

Use these questions below to reflect on your readings this week. Journal your answers and/or process them with your small group.

Which person did you most identify with this week?

What was your connection?

Which person do you believe had to dig deepest to find hope? Why?

What is left unhealed in your life?

How did the hope of each story perhaps provide a pathway in your journey towards hope and healing?

As you journey through Advent and look towards the new year, what will you be taking with you as a result of this week's study?

WEEK TWO

Opportunity and Love

Second Sunday of Advent

And now these three remain: faith, hope and love.
But the greatest of these is love.

1 Corinthians 13:13 (NIV)

I'll never forget the first moment that I held my son in my arms after friends and family left the hospital room for the night. I looked at him, and my first reaction was fear. "Oh my goodness," I thought, "I'm a mother now... and I don't know what I'm doing! How can they leave me here alone with this helpless baby?"

Then I looked at this precious baby sleeping in my arms and I was overwhelmed with love. The fear subsided, and all I could do was stare at this precious gift of a child I immediately loved so profoundly. When my daughter was born a few years later, I wondered if my love would now be divided between my two children, but it just multiplied. Love multiplies, love casts out fear, love comforts and guides us in all situations. Love is the greatest gift we can receive and the greatest gift we can offer to others on life's journey.

Sometimes we confuse love and gifts during the Christmas season. We think that the quality or quantity of gifts that we give will prove our love for others.

- Love is a gift that can't be wrapped and put in a box.
- Love can't be purchased with a credit card.
- Love is something we need to give and receive each day.
- Love is lived out in our actions.

The story of Jesus' birth is full of love. Mary's love for God, Zechariah and Elizabeth's love for John the Baptist, Joseph's love for Mary, God's love for the Shepherds and for all of us who have heard the good news of Jesus' birth!

As you spend this week learning more about love, ask yourself how you can show love to others every single day. Put your love in action and see how God uses you to bring the light of love into the lives of others this Advent season!

Reflections from Day One

1. How can you share the gift of love rather than a physical gift this year?

2. How might you ask to share experiences with loved ones rather than exchange gifts this Advent season?

3. How might you express an extra helping of self-love this season?

Monday

Zechariah

> *But the angel said to him: "Do not be afraid,*
> *Zechariah; your prayer has been heard. Your wife*
> *Elizabeth will bear you a son, and you are to call*
> *him John. Zechariah asked the angel, "How can*
> *I be sure of this? I am an old man and my wife is*
> *well along in years." The angel said to him, "I am*
> *Gabriel. I stand in the presence of God, and I have*
> *been sent to speak to you and to tell you this good*
> *news. And now you will be silent and not able to*
> *speak until the day this happens, because you did*
> *not believe my words, which will come true at their*
> *appointed time."*
>
> **Luke 1:13,18-20 (NIV)**

Have you ever received news that seemed too good to be true? Zechariah and his wife had waited decades to become parents, and now an angel is telling Zechariah that a baby boy is on the way. Part of me can understand Zechariah's disbelief at this shocking news, and I wondered why Zechariah was struck silent for the duration of Elizabeth's pregnancy because of his reaction. But then I realized that when I feel God is telling me something hard to believe, the best initial response is silence.

In Luke 2:19, we read that Mary's reaction to Jesus' birth was silence as she "treasured all these things in her heart." My first reaction to exciting news and events is to talk about it! But when I close my mouth and take time to ponder the news I'm hearing, I'm better able to reflect on who God is and what God is doing instead of how impossible it may feel. The good news is that we serve a God of the impossible. A God who brings life from death, healing from brokenness, joy from sorrow. We serve a God who initiated the salvation of the world through the birth of a vulnerable baby.

Zechariah had months of silence to reflect on what God was doing through the birth of his son, John. Advent is a busy season for many of us, and it may feel like taking a few moments of silence each day is impossible. But I hope that you take some time during this season of Advent to be silent and ponder what God was doing through the birth of Jesus. Take this opportunity to see God's extravagant love and grace that was born that night in Bethlehem and reflect upon it. And by doing so, may you receive the gift of God's abiding love as the best Christmas gift of all!

Reflections from Day Two

1. In these days leading up to the celebration of the birth of Jesus, on what might you reflect and ponder?

2. How might this intentional time of silence and reflection add to your sense of hope in this Advent season?

3. How will you "gift" yourself this time with God receiving his unconditional abiding love?

Tuesday

Mary

*About that time Caesar Augustus ordered a census
to be taken throughout the Empire. This was
the first census when Quirinius was governor of
Syria. Everyone had to travel to his own ancestral
hometown to be accounted for. So Joseph went from
the Galilean town of Nazareth up to Bethlehem
in Judah, David's town, for the census. As a
descendant of David, he had to go there. He went
with Mary, his fiancée, who was pregnant.*

*While they were there, the time came for her to
give birth. She gave birth to a son, her firstborn.
She wrapped him in a blanket and laid him in a
manger, because there was no room in the hostel.*

Luke 2:1-7 (TM)

Many of us have had the honor and privilege of
holding a newborn baby. Maybe you have also been a
part of the miracle of childbirth. Words can't describe
it! It's a holy moment. Can you imagine how Mary
must have felt? It's an overwhelming experience to
bring new life into the world, but can you imagine

giving birth to savior of humanity? Talk about overwhelming!

When holding infants in your arms, you can't help but wonder how this person will impact the world. You can't help but wonder what kind of person this baby will become. But imagine Mary looking into the eyes of her newborn child already knowing He has been purposely placed in her arms to raise and will go on to save people from their sins. The love Mary must have felt! The opportunity Mary knew (at least to some degree) was laying in her arms! It is hard to imagine being in Mary's sandals.

As you reflect on your life's journey, when have you experienced an overwhelming sense of love? Let the memory wash over you as though you were experiencing it anew. Take a moment to journal your thoughts and feelings. Are there any walls that need to be examined in your life that might be blocking opportunities for love? If so, journal these thoughts. How might you open your heart up in this coming year for more opportunities and loving experiences?

Reflections from Day Three

1. How have you experienced an overwhelming sense of love? If so, reflect on your experience. If not, reflect on what blocks might be in your way of these possible experiences.

2. How might you create that experience of overwhelming love for someone dear to you?

3. How might creating that experience for someone else fill you with a sense of joy and love in return?

Wednesday

Joseph

Then Joseph woke up. He did exactly what God's angel commanded in the dream:
He married Mary.

Matthew 1:24 (TM)

Joseph was already in love with Mary. They had already planned to be married. But then this thing happened that caused him to pause. Mary was pregnant, but it was not Joseph's baby. How could he marry Mary, who was carrying another man's baby? He must have felt betrayed. He was trying to find a way out of these circumstances. But then this Angel appeared in his dream and explained the situation to him. When he awoke from his dream, he proceeded to marry Mary as planned.

Weddings are usually full of emotion. Most of the time, the primary feeling is love. When the eyes of the groom and bride meet for the first time as the bride makes her way down the aisle is always anticipated. The onlookers are often reminiscing about a similar personal situation. They may remember feelings of overwhelming love for a person themselves. It is one of the most profound feelings we can experience - love.

Imagine Joseph as he looked into the eyes of Mary on their wedding day. This woman who he loved is now carrying this extra-special kind of human life. God chose him to be Jesus' earthly father. God chose Mary specifically to birth this child. God hand-picked this couple to raise the son of God. The love Joseph must have felt was surely triple or quadruple the overwhelming love most couples experience on their wedding day.

When have you in your life's journey perhaps been in a situation where you thought you had loved in the most profound way possible only to find an even deeper love? What do you think created the opportunity for this more profound affection? How might this lesson be carried into this journey toward Christmas?

Reflections from Day Four

1. How would you describe "overwhelming love?"

2. When have you experienced overwhelming love? When has love taken your breath away?

3. How will you take time to bask in the love of this Advent season?

Thursday

Shepherds

> *At once the angel was joined by a huge angelic*
> *choir singing God's praises:*
>
> *Glory to God in the heavenly heights,*
>
> *Peace to all men and women on earth who*
> *please him.*
>
> *As the angel choir withdrew into heaven,*
> *the shepherds talked it over. "Let's get over*
> *to Bethlehem as fast as we can and see for*
> *ourselves what God has revealed to us." They*
> *left, running, and found Mary and Joseph,*
> *and the baby lying in the manger. Seeing was*
> *believing. They told everyone they met what the*
> *angels had said about this child. All who heard*
> *the shepherds were impressed.*

Luke 2:13-18 (TM)

Have you ever witnessed someone just giddy with
excitement? Most of us have. When you are in the
presence of people in this state, it is hard not to join
them in their joy or at least smile as you watch them
celebrate. Often when someone is filled with such
excitement, they can't help but share the news or

cause of their giddiness. Think of those parents or grandparents who just can't help themselves when it comes to sharing pictures of their child or grandchild.

The angels appearing to the shepherds shared that they brought good news - fantastic, joyous news. Some might even interpret the story that somewhat of a concert broke out as the angels shared the news and praised God. I imagine the shepherd being giddy with joy and excitement. They couldn't wait to see baby Jesus. They left right away to witness this miracle with their own eyes. After they found Mary and Joseph with baby Jesus, the shepherds spread the good news across the land. The shepherds were given the unique opportunity to be told by the angels, the first to see Jesus, and the ones chosen to carry and spread the news.

When have you been giddy with excitement for the opportunity to share the birth of Jesus? The Christmas story is one of the best "stories" of all time. Yet, so many are unaware of the story, much less the love and opportunity a relationship with Jesus Christ can bring. Maybe it is time for us first to relive the wonderful, joyous news so that we can't wait to share it with others. How will you seize the opportunity and share the wonderful news this Christmas season?

Reflections from Day Five

1. When is the last time you have been giddy with excitement? Describe what about the circumstances made you feel so giddy.

2. During this season of love and joy, how might you create an experience for someone special in your life that might make them feel giddy?

3. How would creating this experience add to the joy of the season for both you and this person?

Friday

Herod

When Herod realized that he had been outwitted by the Magi, he was furious, and he gave orders to kill all the boys in Bethlehem and its vicinity who were two years old and under, in accordance with the time he had learned from the Magi. Then what was said through the prophet Jeremiah was fulfilled:

"A voice is heard in Ramah, weeping and great mourning,

Rachel weeping for her children and refusing to be comforted, because they are no more."

Matthew 2:16-18 (NIV)

Herod is the villain in this story. He is a paranoid, insecure, and evil king who not only murdered members of his own family to preserve his power but he orders every baby boy two years old and younger to be killed in an attempt to murder the "King of the Jews."

King Herod had an opportunity to lead from a place of courage or a place of fear. He could have welcomed this extraordinary baby and protected Jesus' life and purpose, but instead Herod felt threatened and turned to bloodshed to preserve his power.

When I think about the Christmas season, I love to focus on the joy of singing Christmas carols, wrapping gifts for loved ones, and sitting by the Christmas tree while I reflect on the extraordinary birth of Jesus. However, it's equally important for me to realize that even in the story of Jesus' birth, we have evil, sorrow, death and fear. We needed God to come to earth and be born in the flesh because there is so much darkness and despair all around us that we need the light of Christ to guide our way.

As you look around your community, who is struggling with evil, sorrow, death or fear? Who needs to see the light of Christ in you and feel the love of God with your actions? There are people in your neighborhood who feel invisible and alone. There are organizations in your community that need volunteers to help them reach those in pain or distress. Seize this opportunity to make a positive impact on your community, knowing that when you shine the light of Christ to those in need, it is an act of worship to Christ the King.

Reflections from Day Six

1. Who might need some hope and light in this Advent season?

2. How might you offer light and hope?

3. How might your act of lifting another's spirits bring a sense of peace or joy to your own heart?

Saturday

Opportunity& Love

Week Two Summary, Reflection, & Questions

This second week of our journey has taken us into the stories of Jesus' birth through the voices of our characters through love and opportunity.

> *Now we see a reflection in a mirror; then we will see face-to-face. Now I know partially, but then I will know completely in the same way that I have been completely known. Now faith, hope, and love remain – these three things – and the greatest of these is love.*
>
> **1 Corinthians 13:12-13 (CEB)**

Love is often called the universal spiritual gift. While some of our spiritual gifts are unique to us and not shared by all, love is a spiritual gift that must be mixed with all spiritual gifts. We know that love is patient, kind, never fails, isn't jealous, doesn't brag, isn't rude, and doesn't seek its own advantage.

Love puts up with all things, trusts in all things, hopes, for all things, and endures all things.

1 Cor 13:7

We will not truly understand love in its depth until we are with Jesus.

Use these questions below to reflect on your readings this week. Journal your answers and/or process them with your small group.

How has your understanding of love evolved in your life's journey?

For you, how do opportunity and love go hand in hand?

What opportunities are before you in this Advent season and as you enter into a new year?

What would a deeper love look like for you in this Advent season?

If we express our faith in God by loving others, how does this reflection play into how we desire to show up in the new year?

WEEK THREE

Peace

Third Sunday of Advent

If there's one word that I would not use to describe the season of Advent, it is "peaceful." My husband and I are both pastors and we have two young children, so the month of December is full of endless activities that can leave us exhausted and overwhelmed on Christmas morning. Sometimes I get so focused on the busyness of the Advent season that the last thing I seem to experience is peace.

In Hebrew, a word for peace is shalom. But shalom isn't just the absence of conflict or fighting, the root of the word means wholeness or completeness. Peace, in this sense, is being in a right relationship with God, with yourself, and with others. To have peace is to have wholeness and completeness in who you are and in how you interact with others.

I don't know about you, but I could use a lot more shalom in my life! How would this Christmas be different if what we sought, more than anything else, was shalom in the relationships that matter most to us? During the Covid-19 pandemic, many of us realized that the relationships with those we cared about were stronger or not as strong as we expected. How might this Advent be different if we intentionally created more space for peace in our relationships? What if we set aside time each day to be with the ones we love?

Whether it is taking the time to engage this devotional and spend time in prayer with God or having a great conversation with a friend or family member, the more intentional time you invest in relationships, the stronger they can become. But the only way to have the added time to invest in these relationships is to set boundaries with our schedules. What do we have to do less of to have more time with those we love? How can we set healthier boundaries this year to experience the deep shalom, the wholeness that we have been longing for?

The devotions for this week will help you explore what the presence or absence of peace looks like through the voices of these Biblical characters.

Reflections from Day One

1. Describe what a sense of peace or "shalom" means to you.

2. How are you experiencing a sense of, or lack of, peace this season? Describe where you are at this moment in your sense of peacefulness.

3. How will you intentionally create a more profound sense of peace in this Advent season?

Monday

Zechariah

He asked for a writing tablet, and to everyone's astonishment he wrote, "His name is John." Immediately his mouth was opened and his tongue set free, and he began to speak, praising God.

Luke 1:63-64 (NIV)

After nine months of silence, Zechariah was able to speak again! Imagine the peace and joy that he experienced when he cried out, "His name is to be John." Zechariah's first words were words of obedience to the angel Gabriel's message to name his son John. After he showed his obedience, he was led to praise God and prophecy about what John would do.

Zechariah ends his prophecy with these words:

Then showing us the way, one foot at a time, down the path of peace.

Luke 1:79

58

Peace is a process. Peace is a journey. You might have peaceful moments in your life, but to experience peace, you need to take one step at a time down the path of peace. How do we do that? Zechariah models some of those steps for us as we read of his obedience to live into the promises God has made. We move down the path of peace when we live by the promises God makes to us in obedience.

We also move down the path towards peace when we worship God. How? In worship, we are reminded of God's greatness and goodness, and we seek to live in shalom with God and others. We want the right relationships and wholeness between ourselves and God. Zechariah's son would prepare the people for Jesus by reminding them that peace with God comes from acknowledging our brokenness and turning to God for wholeness and healing.

Are you experiencing peace in your life? Why or why not? How could the steps of obedience and worship help you take that next step? What steps of peace would you like to take in your journey towards Christmas?

Reflections from Day Two

1. How would you describe the steps in your peacefulness pathway?

2. How far along are you in your peacefulness pathway?

3. What is the next faithful step in your pathway of peacefulness?

Tuesday

Mary

Then they returned to Jerusalem from the mount
called Olivet, which is near Jerusalem, a sabbath
day's journey away.

When they had entered the city, they went to the
room upstairs where they were staying, Peter,
and John, and James, and Andrew, Philip and
Thomas, Bartholomew and Matthew, James son
of Alphaeus, and Simon the Zealot, and Judas,
son of James.

All these were constantly devoting themselves to
prayer, together with certain women, including
Mary the mother of Jesus, as well as his brothers.

Acts 1:12-14 (NRSV)

This group of faithful followers of Jesus had just
witnessed the ascension of Jesus into heaven. They
had returned to Jerusalem and gathered once again.
It goes on to tell us that they had been "constantly
devoting themselves to prayer." Among this group is
Mary, the mother of Jesus. This woman had seen her
son crucified and buried. Some believe she was the
"other Mary" with Mary Magdalene, who discovered

the empty tomb. This poor mother had endured so much, and here she was in the upper room with mostly men and "certain women."

Yet, with all the horribleness she had endured, one can't help but think that Mary must have finally had a peace about her. This baby that she birthed, raised, loved, and followed had fulfilled the prophecy of which she and others had been told. Her son was no longer suffering. Her son would live at the right hand of God forever. Her son was with his Father in heaven. How much of a more profound sense of peace can there be?

During this Advent season, how would you describe your sense of peace? Are you experiencing peace through the hope and love the season celebrates? Or is your depth of peace feeling a bit shallow? How might you wade deeper into the peace that Christ offers each one of us during this Christmas season? How is God calling you into His loving arms and offering you peace and solace in your journey?

Reflections from Day Three

1. How can reflecting on the story and miracle of the birth of Christ add to your sense of peace?

2. How could reflecting on the unconditional love that Christ offers increase your sense of peace?

3. Reflect on the peace Mary must have felt when she knew her son, Jesus, was sitting at the right hand of God. How must that have felt?

Wednesday

Joseph

Later, when Herod died, God's angel appeared in a
dream to Joseph in Egypt: "Up, take the child and
his mother and return to Israel. All those out to
murder the child are dead."

Matthew 2:19-20 (CEB)

After the shepherds visited baby Jesus, an angel
appeared to Joseph, telling him to take Mary and
Jesus and escape to Egypt. King Herod wanted Jesus
dead. Imagine having this Savior baby placed in your
custody for care and protection and then hearing this
kind of news. Imagine what the journey to Egypt must
have been like. The worry, anxiety, being on guard,
and unable to rest must have been overwhelming. But
even in Egypt, I can imagine still being a bit antsy
and on edge knowing Herod wanted your son killed.

Then the angel appeared to Joseph and told him
it was safe to return to Israel. The king who wanted

Jesus dead is now dead himself! That was probably the longest exhale Joseph had taken in quite some time. One can only imagine Joseph's sense of relief – the sense of peace. Knowing the one who wanted your son dead is no longer a threat must have brought a deep sense of tranquility and serenity.

When you think of peace, what comes to mind for you? What brings you the most profound sense of peace? What is your level of peacefulness in this season of Advent? How could you reach deeper into the hope and peace of Jesus as you journey into this new year?

Reflections from Day Four

1. Reflect on a time when some news instantly brought you relief and a sense of peace. How would you describe that sense of peacefulness?

2. How do you remind yourself to place your worries and concerns in Jesus's hands instead of carrying those yourself and rob your sense of peacefulness?

3. How does your body respond to stress or lack of peacefulness? When you sense this stress in your body, what strategies do you use to relax and relieve this stress to regain your sense of peace?

Thursday

Shepherds

The shepherds returned home, glorifying and praising God for all they had heard and seen. Everything happened just as they had been told.

Luke 2:20 (CEB)

The shepherds had heard from the angels that Jesus had been born. They left their sheep and immediately went to see for themselves. When they arrived, they witnessed everything precisely as it was told it would be. They shared what they had been told with Mary and Joseph. They left, returned home, and praised God.

The Savior was born . . . their Savior was born. And, they got to witness the whole thing! These shepherds had longed for, waited for, and yearned for the arrival of a Savior. The time had come. This baby lying in a manger is Christ the Lord. Imagine the peace these shepherds must have felt. Finally, He is here. Finally, we will be saved! Even the angels proclaimed to the shepherds, "Peace to all men and women on earth who please him." (Luke 2:14 MSG) What a peaceful night of rest those shepherds must have enjoyed when they returned home!

Sometimes in the season of Advent, we find ourselves in a hectic schedule of shopping, wrapping, cooking, entertaining, decorating, and such. In the hubbub of activity, we often miss the sense of peace in celebrating Jesus' birth.

How are you experiencing peace in the midst of this season? What brings you a sense of peace? What distracts you from your sense of peace? How will you more intentionally make space for the peace of the season? How will you carry this also into the new year?

Reflections from Day Five

1. How is the busy-ness of the season robbing you of your peace?

2. What strategies will you use to retain a sense of peace in this Advent season?

3. What strategies will help you during the upcoming year?

Friday

Wise Men

*After Jesus was born in Bethlehem in Judea,
during the time of King Herod, Magi from the east
came to Jerusalem and asked, "Where is the one
who has been born king of the Jews? We saw his
star when it rose and have come to worship him."
When King Herod heard this he was disturbed,
and all Jerusalem with him.*

Matthew 2:1-3 (NIV)

What happens when the good news isn't good news
to you? Magi from the east come to Jerusalem, looking
for the king of the Jews. "King Herod heard this he
was disturbed, and all Jerusalem with him." Why
were they disturbed? There had been prophecies that
a king would be coming who would bring peace to the
Jews, and it seems as if the prophecy is being fulfilled.
That's not just good news. That's great news!

The Greek word for "disturbed" means stirring up
or agitating something, like when you stir water in
a pool. So perhaps King Herod and all of Jerusalem

were "stirred up" because they didn't realize the significance of the star. When there are vivid signs that something miraculous has occurred and you aren't the first to know, it can make you anxious about other signs you may have missed.

Or perhaps they were stirred up because it meant that things would change. A new king had been born. Sometimes, when we face change at home, at work, or in the church, it can agitate us and keep us from seeing the good news in our midst.

Another reason they could have been stirred up because this was a situation they could not control and might lead to a loss of power for King Herod. When we feel like we are losing control or power in a situation, it can lead to great agitation.

Have you felt agitated or disturbed lately? Has this season of Advent stirred up something in you? Do you feel like you are missing out on something? Is change coming that you cannot control that makes you feel powerless? Take some time to reflect on what you are feeling and determine if these feelings keep you from seeing and living into good news as you journey to Christmas.

Reflections from Day Six

1. Sometimes, we "lose" our routine during the Advent season, which might cause us some agitation. What is the rating on your agitation meter this week?

Normal
Routine

Totally
Agitated

2. Sometimes there are family dynamics that make life difficult during the Christmas season. Does this resonate with you? If so, reflect on those feelings and how you might respond in healthier ways.

3. When you experience feelings of agitation or being out of control, how do you typically respond? Is it healthy? If not, how would you like to improve your response?

Saturday

Peace

This week we have journeyed through the voices of our characters in their experiences of peace. While each experienced peace uniquely, each is an integral part of the Advent story. Peace is a state of being, a state of mind, and a feeling. Most everyone desires a life of peace. Yet, we often create a life (knowingly or not) that drains us of our sense of peace. We pray this week has lent itself to an opportunity to consider your sense of peace and perhaps even reach for a deeper sense of peace during this journey towards the hope in Christmas.

Use these questions below to reflect on your readings this week. Journal your answers or process them with your small group.

What has this journey in experiencing peace with our characters brought up for you?

How has your understanding of peace shifted as a result of your study and reflection this week?

Which character do you most identify with this week? Why?

How would you describe your level of peacefulness during this Advent season?

What would you like to take with you in terms of peacefulness into the new year?

WEEK FOUR

Experience and Joy

Fourth Sunday of Advent

Intro

Count it all joy, my brothers, when you meet trials of various kinds, for you know that the testing of your faith produces steadfastness. And let steadfastness have its full effect, that you may be perfect and complete, lacking in nothing.

James 1:2-4 (ESV)

Jesus may have been Mary's firstborn son, but he would not be her last. James, Jesus' younger half-brother, wrote the words above. When Jesus began his ministry, James wasn't sure that his big brother was the Son of God (John 7:5), but he came to believe and was a follower of Jesus. In these verses, James is reminding us that joy should not be dependent on our circumstances.

If joy comes from material possessions or power or a perfect life, then our joy is dependent on the situations around us. True joy is a condition of the heart, and it comes from knowing that God will use all of the situations we face, both good and bad, to help us grow and mature in our faith.

Did Mary think that she would get pregnant out of wedlock and give birth to a child surrounded by animals far from her home? Did Joseph believe that he would have to flee as an immigrant to Egypt to protect the lives of his family?

Sometimes the situations we have to face aren't what we expect. Yet, we can experience joy in all circumstances when we remind ourselves that God is present with us and has a plan to guide us through whatever we might face.

Perhaps this last year was difficult for you, and you haven't felt the same amount of joy that you usually do as Christmas approaches. Take heart. Christmas is almost here!

As you celebrate the birth of Jesus, may you be reminded that Christ's ongoing gift of the Holy Spirit lives in you and can bring you joy no matter what situations come your way. Hold onto hope, embrace joy, and continue to move forward in your journey of faith!

Reflections from Day One

1. Reflect on the statement, "true joy is a condition of the heart." How is the condition of your heart?

2. If true joy comes from knowing God uses all things for helping us grow in our faith, how have you joyfully grown in faith through both pleasant and challenging situations in the past year?

3. How do you remind yourself of the ongoing Holy Spirit's guidance through whatever circumstances life throws in your path?

DAY TWO

Monday

Elizabeth

*When Elizabeth heard Mary's greeting, the baby
in her womb leaped. She was filled with the Holy
Spirit, and sang out exuberantly,*

*You're so blessed among women, and the babe in
your womb, also blessed!*

*And why am I so blessed that the mother of my
Lord visits me?*

*The moment the sound of your greeting entered my
ears,*

*The babe in my womb skipped like a lamb for
sheer joy.*

*Blessed woman, who believed what God said,
believed every word would come true!*

Luke 1:40-45 (TM)

Think about the last time you shared good news
with a friend. How did they respond? Were they
excited for you, or did they try to compete with good
news of their own? Did they share in your joy or get
jealous? When it comes to friendship, I want to be like
Elizabeth! When Mary visits her, John the Baptist

leaps for joy in Elizabeth's belly, leading Elizabeth to sing out a celebration of Mary and her faithfulness.

Elizabeth could have been jealous of Mary. Elizabeth could have wondered why Mary was the chosen mother of God's son. But instead, Elizabeth experiences joy and supports her friend as they share in their pregnancy journeys together.

Elizabeth and Zechariah had been married for decades and longed for a child before Elizabeth became pregnant with John the Baptist in her old age. But Mary was still young, unwed, and probably scared about what would happen to her and this life inside of her. Elizabeth's encouragement and friendship were a gift to Mary in uncertain times. Elizabeth's son would also be a friend to Jesus, preparing the way for Jesus' ministry and later baptizing Jesus in the River Jordan.

Think about your friendships in your life's journey. How have friends been supportive along the way? How can you be supportive and encouraging of your friends? What can you celebrate together?

Reflections from Day Two

1. What dear friend in your life brings you pure joy?

2. How does this friend bring joy to your life?

3. Reach out to your dear friend and express your gratitude for the joy they bring to your life.

Tuesday

Mary

Two days later Jesus' mother was a guest at a wedding in the village of Cana in Galilee, and Jesus and his disciples were invited too. During the festivities, the wine supply ran out, and Jesus' mother came to him with the problem.

"I can't help you now," he said, "It isn't yet my time for miracles."

But his mother told the servants, "Do whatever he tells you to."

John 2:1-5 (TLB)

Mary was the first to notice that the couple was about to run out of wine. What an embarrassment this would be for the couple. Running out of wine would likely signify that they did not have enough money to provide for the guests they had invited. Mary also knew the ministry Jesus was to have and had waited nearly thirty years to see it come to fruition. While Jesus wasn't sure it was his time to start his ministry, Mary encouraged him, and he responded.

Mary helped launch Jesus' ministry at the wedding by turning water into wine.

Imagine waiting and watching all those years. Imagining what could be, what would be. While Mary had seen glimpses of what Jesus' ministry might become, I am sure she was anxious to see it come to fruition. With a mother's heart, she noticed an opportunity for a young couple to be spared embarrassment on their special day, and as a result, her son's ministry as an adult began . . . at a wedding . . . making wine from water. Imagine the joy she must have felt to see this!

We don't always get to witness all the joyous occasions of our children (or grandchildren, nieces, or nephews), especially in their adult years. For Mary to be there with him must have brought her great pleasure beyond our imagination.

In this Advent season, how are you experiencing pure joy? Where are you delighting in the Lord? Where are you finding happiness as we celebrate the birth of Christ? What is distracting you from the joy of the season? How might you eliminate or lessen those distractions in your journey of hope towards Christmas?

Reflections from Day Three

1. How are you delighting in the Lord in this season?

2. Often, we are swept up in all the preparations and activities of the season and miss the opportunities to notice moments of joy. Perhaps it's a child's awe in the lights on the tree or a grandparent's joy in sitting at the table on Christmas surrounded by family. How are you slowing down during Advent to delight in experiencing the joy in others?

3. What is distracting you from experiencing this delight, and how will you seek to lessen or remove this distraction?

Wednesday

Joseph

The next day they found him in the Temple seated among the teachers, listening to them and asking questions. The teachers were all quite taken with him, impressed with the sharpness of his answers. But his parents were not impressed; they were upset and hurt.

His mother said, "Young man, why have you done this to us? Your father and I have been half out of our minds looking for you."

He said, "Why were you looking for me? Didn't you know that I had to be here, dealing with the things of my Father?" But they had no idea what he was talking about.

So he went back to Nazareth with them, and lived obediently with them. His mother held these things dearly, deep within herself. And Jesus matured, growing up in both body and spirit, blessed by both God and people.

Luke 2:46-52 (TM)

Joseph and Mary had lost track of Jesus. They thought he was with some other families as they traveled back from Jerusalem after the Feast of the

Passover. When they realized he was missing, they circled back to Jerusalem and found him in the Temple. While the teachers were impressed with Jesus' answers, his parents were not impressed with his choice to stay behind. They had been worried, upset and hurt by his decision.

While being upset with Jesus was quite understandable, one can't help but wonder that Joseph might have felt something different after he knew Jesus was okay. Knowing what Jesus came to offer the world, Joseph was likely pretty proud of his son, too. There must have been joy in seeing the young Jesus following His Heavenly Father at such a young age and impressing those teachers. Maybe there was joy in this experience, too.

We can define "joy" as delight, exuberance, and blissfulness. In this season of Advent, how are you finding blissfulness in the Lord? What are you planning to celebrate with joyful exuberance intentionally? What sense of joy will you take with you on your journey into the new year?

Reflections from Day Four

1. When was the last time you used the word "exuberance?" Even the word itself is fun and full of possibility. Create an experience that would result in the feeling of exuberance.

2. Share the experience you created with a friend.

3. Challenge the friend to repeat the process of creating such an experience.

Thursday

Shepherds

As the shepherds returned to their sheep, they were praising God and saying wonderful things about him. Everything they had seen and heard was just as the angel had said.

Luke 2:20 (CEV)

The lives of the shepherds were changed forever. The angels had come to share the good news with them. They were some of the first to know. They were some of the first to see Jesus. They got the joy of telling Mary and Joseph about the appearance of the angels and what they had shared. They left a lasting impression on Mary by sharing the angel's message with her.

They were able to tell all that would listen about all the wonderful things they had experienced. The announcement to the shepherds was a unique, once-in-a-lifetime experience that only they shared.

The shepherds saw Jesus long before the magi. Jesus was less than a week old, still in the manger, when the shepherds first laid eyes on the baby Jesus. Filled with joy from the entire experience, they were the first evangelists. One can only imagine how the local townspeople people spoke of the shepherds' experience often.

When a new person was in town, the local folks would joyfully introduce their shepherd friends as "my good buddy who was visited by angels who shared that our Savior had been born. He was one of the first actually to lay eyes on Jesus."

The shepherds were likely the local celebrities. The shepherds were not looking to be famous or be struck by stardom. The shepherds were simply out in the fields doing their work of tending to their sheep. It was likely a night like most others until it wasn't. Their life changed forever in a moment.

When have you ever had a surprising experience that left you with unexpected joy? It is sometimes in those serendipitous moments that bring solid memories and emotions. Journal as many details as you can remember about the experience. What was it about the experience that brought you such joy? How are you experiencing that joy in reminiscing about the memory? How might you share that type of joy with someone else during this Advent season?

Reflections from Day Five

1. Describe an unexpected experience that left you with unexpected joy.

2. Describe another unexpected experience that left you with unexpected joy.

3. Challenge yourself all week to either remember an experience from the past or notice something from the day that brought you an unexpected element of joy. You just might be surprised at how many joyful moments you were missing when you weren't paying attention.

Friday

The Wise Men

> *Instructed by the king, they set off. Then the star appeared again, the same star they had seen in the eastern skies. It led them on until it hovered over the place of the child.*
>
> *They could hardly contain themselves: They were in the right place! They had arrived at the right time! They entered the house and saw the child in the arms of Mary, his mother. Overcome, they kneeled and worshiped him.*
>
> **Matthew 2:9-11 (TM)**

Every time I look at my nativity set with the baby Jesus in a manger and the wise men kneeling around him with gifts of gold, frankincense and myrrh, I smile. It might comfort us to think of the wise men worshiping the baby Jesus, but they weren't there the night of his birth or even the week of his birth. They even missed his first birthday. It took a couple of years for the wise men to travel from where they lived, perhaps in Babylon or Persia, to Bethlehem.

In verse 11, we read that they entered the house

where Jesus was staying, he wasn't in a stable anymore:

They entered the house and saw the child in the arms of Mary, his mother.

The wise men saw a star in the sky and set out on a pilgrimage that lasted well over a year, traveling to see the King of the Jews. I'm comforted by the reminder that sometimes when we are seeking to encounter Christ, it takes time.

It's a journey. There are some days during the Advent season when I wake up singing carols and am full of exuberant joy as if it were Christmas morning. But there are other days when I feel like the wise men, still traveling and seeking to find Christ amid a busy and chaotic season.

Another powerful reminder from the story of the wise men is that they weren't Jewish. These astrologers from a foreign land had a deep desire to worship Jesus, King of the Jews, and were welcomed into Jesus' home.

If you feel like an outsider of faith or have ever felt like you didn't belong somewhere, the story of the wise men is a reminder that Jesus' birth unites us all, and we all have a place in the story. As you continue to seek Christ this Advent season, do you feel like you are still on a journey to experience joy? In what ways can you share the story of Jesus' birth with those who might feel like "outsiders" and welcome them in with love and hospitality?

Reflections from Day Six

1. Our faith walk is a journey – sometimes difficult and other times smooth. Reflect on how you would currently describe your faith journey.

2. As you reflect on your faith journey, what joy moments can you identify, now or in the past, to celebrate during this season?

3. Is there someone that God might be calling you to share the Good News with during this season? If so, who? How might you consider sharing?

Saturday

Experience & Joy

In our fourth and final week of this journey, we spent time experiencing joy through the voices and lives of our characters from the Advent story. The birth of Jesus is the epitome of the deepest expression of joy. We pray you have experienced such joy in this week of Christmas.

Use these questions below to reflect on your readings this week. Journal your answers and/or process them with your small group.

Which character did you most identify with this week in their experience of joy? Why?

How has reflecting on joy in this week of Christmas perhaps opened your eyes more deeply to the joy of Advent?

What circumstances, people, activities, etc., in your life steal your joy? What might you do to eliminate this?

Gabrielle Roy says, "The more the heart is sated with joy, the more it becomes insatiable." How does this quote speak to you in this week of Christmas?

How will you intentionally pursue a life that brings you the deepest joy as you begin your journey into the new year?

POSTSCRIPT
A Plan of Hope

A Plan of HOPE

During this Advent season, we have listened to the voices of six unique characters each week through a lens of HOPE in healing, opportunity, peace, and experience as we cast our eyes towards hope, love, peace, and joy in this season of the birth of the baby Jesus. Each character brought their unique perspectives, voices, and insights as we hope you have done the same.

Just like the characters in the Advent story, each of us encounters the season of Advent in a unique way, growing from the experiences in our own life journeys. We pray this resource and – if you participated in this study with a group – your small group experience has multiplied your hope, love, peace, and joy this Advent season.

As you close in on Advent and enter into another new year, take some time to reflect on how you might want to enter this new year with an intentional renewed sense of HOPE. All of us could use a bit more HOPE in our life's journey.

What is your HOPE plan for the coming year?

Take some time, using the space on the following pages, to create your *PLAN OF HOPE.* You might even consider making a vision board to help turn your plan into reality.

According to *Psychology Today,* mental practices (like visualization) can increase motivation, confidence, and even motor performance. In fact, in one study researchers found, in athletes, visualization was almost as effective as physical practice.

Google "vision board" for inspiration and assistance in creating a vision board.[1]

PLAN OF HOPE

HEALING

How will this new year be a year of healing?

What will be healed in your life during this new year?

---

[1] oprahdaily.com/life/a29959841/how-to-make-a-vision-board

How will you step into this healing with intention and patience?

How will this healing bring a new sense of hope within you?

OPPORTUNITY

What new opportunities will you pursue in this new year?

How is God calling you into this new year?

How are you being led into a new or deeper sense of love? How is this opportunity part of your God-provided purpose?

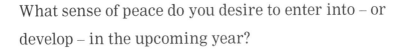
PEACE

What sense of peace do you desire to enter into – or develop – in the upcoming year?

How will you pursue this sense of peace with purpose, intention, and patience?

How will this sense of peace bring a renewed sense of hope within you?

How might a deepened relationship with God bring you a deeper sense of peace?

EXPERIENCE

What new experiences will you enjoy in this upcoming year?

What experiences will you begin, continue, or renew that bring a pure sense of joy?

What people bring you joy?

Are you spending time with those that bring you joy and minimizing the time with people who steal your joy?

How does spending time with God daily bring you joy?

How does experiencing a deepening relationship with God bring you a sense of joy?

Final Recommendations

We recommend spending some intentional and quality time preparing your Plan of Hope. Pray for your Plan of Hope and pray over your Plan of Hope. Consider creating a Plan of Hope Vision Board to bring clarity and momentum to lean into and activate your Plan of Hope.

If you are participating in a small group, your group might even consider gathering again to share your *Plans of Hope* (whether they are written, oral, or on vision boards). Sharing your Plans of Hope brings them another step closer towards reality. And even better, pray over one another's Plans of Hope.

You may even decide to check in on one another from time to time to see how God is intersecting in your small group participants' lives and Plans of Hope. Heck, you may just decide to continue to gather regularly and become an ongoing HOPE Small Group to pray together, share hope-filled scripture, and hold one another accountable for living out your Plans of Hope. Only God knows what could be possible.

We pray this has been a hope-filled experience for you during this Advent season. May this investment in your discipleship journey be a blessing to you!

With deep and heartfelt prayers,

Rachel & Kay

New Titles
from Market Square Books

2022 Lenten Study
Journey to Transformation
Bishop Sharma Lewis

2021 Advent Study
HOPE: An Advent Journey
Olu Brown

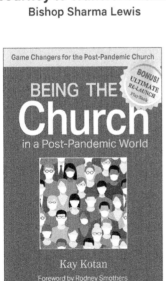

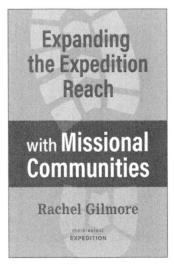

Being the Church
in a Post-Pandemic World
Kay Kotan

Expanding the Expedition
with Missional Communities
Rachel Gilmore

More Titles
from Market Square Books
marketsquarebooks.com

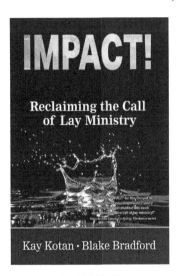

IMPACT!
Reclaiming the Call of Lay Ministry
Kay Kotan • Blake Bradford

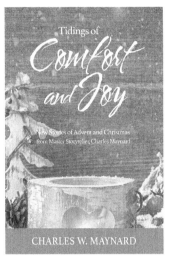

Tidings of Comfort and Joy
Charles W. Maynard

Lenten Study: ATONE
The Difference the Cross Makes
Wil Cantrell

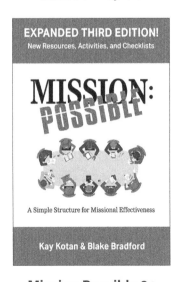

Mission Possible 3+
A Simple Structure for Missional Effectiveness
Kay Kotan & Blake Bradford

Great Study Books
for your small group or class
marketsquarebooks.com

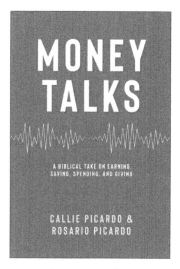

Money Talks
A Biblical Take on Earning,
Saving, Spending, and Giving

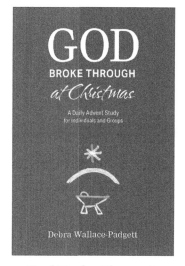

God Broke Through
at Christmas
Bishop Debra Wallace-Padgett

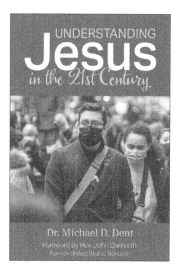

Understanding Jesus
in the 21st Century
Dr. Michael D. Dent

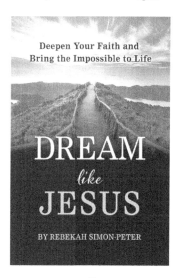

Dream Like Jesus
Deepen Your Faith and Bring
the Impossible to Life

Made in the USA
Middletown, DE
23 October 2021